Don't Say That!

By Janine Amos   Illustrated by Annabel Spenceley

Consultant Rachael Underwood

Gareth Stevens Publishing
A WORLD ALMANAC EDUCATION GROUP COMPANY

Please visit our web site at: www.garethstevens.com
For a free color catalog describing Gareth Stevens Publishing's
list of high-quality books and multimedia programs, call
1-800-542-2595 (USA) or 1-800-387-3178 (Canada).
Gareth Stevens Publishing's fax: (414) 332-3567.

Library of Congress Cataloging-in-Publication Data

Amos, Janine.
    Don't say that! / by Janine Amos; illustrated by Annabel Spenceley.
        p. cm. — (Courteous kids)
    Includes bibliographical references.
    Summary: Two brief stories demonstrate the importance of avoiding mocking
and careless speech when we speak to one another.
    ISBN 0-8368-3606-5 (lib. bdg.)
    1. Interpersonal communication—Juvenile literature. [1. Behavior. 2. Etiquette.
3. Conduct of life.] I. Spenceley, Annabel, ill. II. Title.
BF637.C45.A65   2003
177'.1—dc21   2002036500

This edition first published in 2003 by
Gareth Stevens Publishing
A World Almanac Education Group Company
330 West Olive Street, Suite 100
Milwaukee, Wisconsin 53212 USA

3 1984 00204 7510

Series editor: Dorothy L. Gibbs
Graphic Designer: Katherine A. Goedheer
Cover design: Joel Bucaro

This edition © 2003 by Gareth Stevens, Inc. First published by Cherrytree Press,
a subsidiary of Evans Brothers Limited. © 1999 by Cherrytree (a member of the
Evans Group of Publishers), 2A Portman Mansions, Chiltern Street, London
W1U 6NR, United Kingdom. This U.S. edition published under license from
Evans Brothers Limited. Additional end matter © 2003 by Gareth Stevens, Inc.

Printed in the United States of America

1 2 3 4 5 6 7 8 9 07 06 05 04 03

Note to Parents and Teachers

The questions that appear in **boldface** type can be used to initiate
discussion with your children or class. Encourage them to think of
possible answers before continuing with the story.

Johnny's Dragon

4

Everyone is painting dragons.

Raj paints teeth on his dragon.

Johnny paints all over his paper.

Raj points at Johnny's painting and laughs.

"That's not a dragon!" says Raj.

9

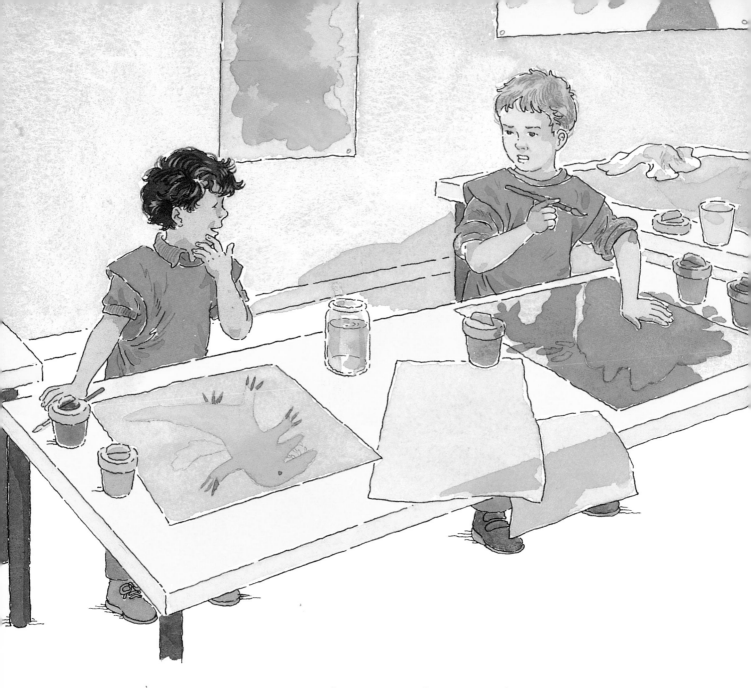

"Don't say that!" Johnny shouts.

"You can't paint a dragon," says Raj.

Johnny throws down his paintbrush and makes a fist.
How do you think Johnny feels?

Steve comes over.
"Stop, Johnny!" he says. "Fighting
is not right. Let's talk about it."

"Raj says my painting isn't a dragon,"
says Johnny.

"It's not right to say that, Raj," says Steve.
How do you think Raj feels?

"You painted your dragon your way," says Steve.
"Johnny painted his dragon his way."

16

"Let's look at all the dragons," says Steve.

"They're all different," says Raj.
"Yes!" Steve agrees. "Everyone has different ideas."
18

Ripe Tomatoes

Katie is at her dad's house.
"What shall we do today?" he asks.

"Are the tomatoes ripe?" asks Katie.
"Can we pick them?"

"Let's take a look!" says Dad.

"Some are ready," he says.
"You start picking. I'll find a bowl."

Katie is excited.
She begins to pick the tomatoes.

She picks more and more.

Her dad comes back with a bowl.
"Stop!" says Dad. "The green
ones aren't ready yet!"

"Oh, I'm stupid!" says Katie.
How do you think Katie feels?

27

"Don't say that!" says Dad.
"It's not true. You just made a mistake."

"But what can we do with the
green ones?" asks Katie.

"No problem," says Dad.
"We can put them on the windowsill.

The sunlight will ripen them."

When people say things you don't like, letting them know is important. Saying "Don't say that!" is one way of telling people to stop and think about what they are saying. If you can, explain why you don't like their words. Then talk about the situation together.

More Books to Read

Be Quiet, Parrot! Jeanne Willis (Carolrhoda Books)

Communication. Aliki (Econo-Clad Books)

The Honest-to-Goodness Truth. Patricia C. McKissack (Atheneum)